Introduction: Scaling Tech Sales in Africa with Limited Resources

Africa represents not just an emerging market but a proving ground for innovation. With over 1.5 billion people, Africa is a mobile-first, fast-growing digital economy. However, challenges like inconsistent infrastructure, diverse regulatory environments, and fragmented markets make it one of the most demanding sales terrains. For sales professionals and leaders, it's not just about selling products—it's about designing solutions that meet local needs and building trust that transcends transactional relationships. The heart of this book lies in giving actionable steps. Whether you're a scrappy startup founder with no CRM or a new sales director building a team, this playbook offers practical advice backed by real-world examples. Here, you'll learn how to navigate these dynamics, overcome hurdles, and thrive in a continent ripe with opportunity.

Throughout this book, we will walk you through proven sales strategies tailored specifically for the African tech market. This is not about abstract theory; it's about practical advice that you can implement immediately. We'll cover everything from building and managing sales pipelines, to navigating the regulatory landscape, to leading high-performance teams despite resource constraints. With real-world examples and case studies drawn from my own experience in tech sales across Africa and my work with startups and global companies, you'll gain insights that will help you thrive—no matter the size of your team, your budget, or your current sales infrastructure.

The journey to scaling tech sales in Africa is one of constant learning and adaptation. In these pages, you'll discover how to tackle common obstacles and unlock growth opportunities in this vast and diverse continent. But it won't be easy. Success in African markets requires grit, perseverance, and a willingness to innovate at every stage of the sales process. However, with the right approach, resources, and mindset, you can transform your sales strategy and contribute to the booming digital economy across the continent. This playbook will guide you through every step of the way, providing you with practical tools and proven strategies to help you succeed, even when resources are limited.

Chapter 1: The African Tech Landscape

To succeed in tech sales in Africa, one must first understand the complexity of the market. Africa is not a monolithic entity; it is a vibrant and diverse continent, rich in opportunity yet fraught with unique challenges. The African digital economy, projected to reach a staggering $712 billion by 2050, is rapidly evolving, and within it, the tech sector is increasingly vital. The fintech space alone attracted over $1.3 billion in funding in 2022, signaling its potential as a driving force for growth. However, the landscape is not without its hurdles—Africa's infrastructure challenges, regulatory inconsistencies, and diverse market needs complicate the journey for tech sales professionals.

In this chapter, we break down how to navigate the African tech sales landscape, beginning with the market dynamics and addressing the specific needs that will shape your sales strategy. Understanding these elements will help you tailor your approach, overcome obstacles, and ultimately thrive in an emerging market that is as promising as it is complex.

Step 1: Understand Market Dynamics

Africa is not a single market, but rather a patchwork of diverse economies, regulations, and business cultures. This makes it critical for any tech sales professional to understand the local dynamics in each country or region where they operate. Whether you are selling SaaS solutions, fintech products, or mobile apps, knowing the local environment is key to aligning your sales strategy with market expectations.

Nigeria:

Nigeria is a leading force in Africa's fintech revolution, with companies like Paystack and Flutterwave attracting global attention. In 2022, Nigeria's fintech industry raised over $500 million, contributing significantly to Africa's overall fintech funding. The country's large population, high smartphone penetration, and relatively low banking penetration present a fertile ground for digital financial solutions. However, Nigeria's regulatory environment can be challenging. The Central Bank of Nigeria (CBN) enforces stringent controls, especially around mobile payments and foreign exchange, which can slow down market entry or complicate operations.

South Africa:

South Africa is one of the more mature economies on the continent with a relatively high level of digital adoption. The country has a well-established banking sector and is a hub for innovation. However, South Africa also has stringent compliance requirements, especially for fintech and tech-based solutions. Companies entering South Africa must be prepared to navigate complex regulations such as the Protection of Personal Information Act (POPIA), which governs data privacy. Despite these challenges, South Africa presents a well-regulated, stable environment for businesses looking to establish a foothold in the Southern African market.

Kenya:

Kenya has long been recognized as a leader in mobile banking, thanks to the success of platforms like M-Pesa. In fact, M-Pesa processes over 45% of Kenya's GDP, making mobile money a central pillar of the economy. This makes Kenya a hotspot for fintech and mobile-based tech solutions. However, infrastructure issues like inconsistent power supply and rural connectivity challenges remain persistent hurdles. A deeper look into mobile usage trends, the impact of mobile money on the economy, and the policies surrounding mobile payments in Kenya will help you tailor your solutions effectively.

Pro Tip: The key to successfully penetrating these diverse markets is to tailor your pitch to local pain points. Start by thoroughly researching the regulatory landscape, economic drivers, and technological barriers in each market. For instance, if you're targeting Nigeria, address concerns around mobile payments, cross-border transactions, and the regulatory hurdles of local partnerships. If you're focusing on Kenya, highlight the mobile-first nature of your product, emphasizing how it integrates with local payment systems like M-Pesa.

Actionable Insight:

Building country-specific customer personas is a highly effective way to understand the local market dynamics and develop personalized sales strategies. Whether it's through interviews with local stakeholders, surveys, or partnerships with local firms, invest in understanding your target market's specific needs before you launch your sales efforts.

Step 2: Overcome Infrastructure Gaps

While Africa's tech potential is undeniable, infrastructure remains a critical challenge. Sub-Saharan Africa has only 43% internet penetration, which can significantly limit your audience's access to your product or service. Additionally, many parts of Africa are still facing significant barriers to reliable power, stable internet connections, and mobile networks. These factors must be accounted for in any sales strategy.

Challenges with Connectivity:

For many regions in Africa, slow internet speeds and intermittent connectivity make it difficult to run cloud-based software, stream content, or manage business operations in real-time. Therefore, sales teams must look at creative ways to work around these limitations. One solution is to offer lightweight, offline-enabled versions of your software or apps. Providing these offline versions will ensure that users in areas with unreliable internet can still access your product.

Collaborate with Telecom Companies:

The role of telecom companies in Africa cannot be overstated. They are the backbone of connectivity on the continent, and forming partnerships with them can help overcome some of the infrastructural challenges. For instance, you might work with telecom companies to offer bundled packages or special data rates for your product. This collaboration could increase user adoption, especially for mobile-first or cloud-based solutions.

Pro Tip:

Collaborating with telecommunications companies can help smooth over the infrastructure gap by ensuring compatibility with local networks and providing potential customers with data packages tailored for your solution. This type of partnership can help scale your product to areas that were previously difficult to reach.

Addressing Customer Support Challenges:

Customer support is another area where Africa's infrastructure gap presents unique challenges. If a large portion of your user base does not have consistent internet access, you must offer multiple ways to connect with support, such as offline chat options, SMS-based troubleshooting, or localized support teams. You also need to create scalable systems that do not require high-speed connections to function effectively.

Step 3: Build Trust

In African markets, relationships are paramount. While other regions may prioritize fast transactions or digital-first sales processes, Africa's business culture places significant weight on building long-term trust. In fact, according to a McKinsey report, 70% of B2B buyers in Africa prefer in-person interactions over digital communication. This preference is rooted in the need to establish strong, trusted relationships, especially for high-value, long-term deals.

Understanding the Importance of In-Person Meetings:

In Africa, selling often goes beyond the product itself—it's about the people behind the product. Trust is built through face-to-face interactions, and this is particularly true when it comes to closing large B2B deals. As a sales leader, you must recognize that while digital channels can open doors, it is often the in-person meeting that solidifies the deal.

Pro Tip: Invest in face-to-face meetings whenever possible. Understand that time spent with a potential client, showing genuine interest in their needs and concerns, can lead to better long-term outcomes. For sales professionals, this means taking the time to visit clients, engaging in small talk, and understanding their businesses on a deeper level.

Building Long-Term Relationships:

Once you've landed the deal, the relationship doesn't end there. Customer retention in Africa is deeply tied to the strength of these relationships. As a result, sales professionals must engage in constant follow-ups, delivering exceptional customer service, and offering solutions that help clients grow. This is especially important in a continent where loyalty is key, and personal rapport can significantly influence repeat business.

Actionable Insight:

To build and maintain trust, ensure you're providing not only excellent customer service but also value-driven solutions that address the long-term needs of your clients. Provide follow-ups and check-ins regularly to ensure they are getting the most out of your product and feel confident in their decision to choose your solution.

By understanding the unique challenges and opportunities in Africa's tech market, you can tailor your sales strategies to meet the needs of local businesses and overcome obstacles in your way. This chapter has introduced the foundational elements of the African tech landscape, but the following chapters will help you dive deeper into specific sales strategies, techniques, and tools that can help you successfully scale in Africa.

Chapter 2: Building Your Sales Pipeline Without a CRM

For many startups across Africa, especially in tech, a Customer Relationship Management (CRM) system is often seen as a luxury. A robust CRM with all the bells and whistles might be far beyond the budget of a small business, yet the importance of tracking your sales pipeline effectively is undeniable. Without proper tracking, you're operating blind. So, what's the solution for startups without access to expensive CRM tools? The answer is simpler and more cost-effective than you might think: Spreadsheets.

Spreadsheets, while basic, can be incredibly powerful when used correctly. They provide a structured way to manage your sales pipeline and are infinitely customizable to meet your specific needs. Let's dive into how you can build and manage your sales pipeline using Google Sheets or Excel to maintain control, track progress, and increase your chances of closing deals.

Step 1: Create a Functional Spreadsheet

Your sales pipeline is the lifeblood of your business. It shows you exactly where every deal stands, which helps prioritize efforts and resources. Here's how to create a functional pipeline spreadsheet using Excel or Google Sheets:

Essential Columns:

- **Lead Name**: The name of the company or individual you're pursuing.
- **Contact Information**: Ensure you have email, phone numbers, and any other contact details.
- **Deal Stage**: A critical piece of data. Categorize your deals in stages such as:

- Discovery (just started)
- Proposal (a formal offer is on the table)
- Negotiation (finalizing the terms)
- Close (deal is done or lost)

- **Deal Value**: The monetary value of the deal. This helps you gauge potential revenue from the pipeline.
- **Expected Close Date**: A target date for when the deal should be closed. This will help you prioritize deals based on time sensitivity.
- **Notes**: Any relevant notes about the lead. For example, special requests, potential blockers, or key decision-makers.

Automation Tips:

- **Weighted Pipeline Value**: A powerful addition is the ability to calculate the weighted value of each deal automatically. For example, if a deal is in the negotiation stage and has a 50% chance of closing, the formula would automatically calculate the value of the deal based on this probability. The formula would be something like: `Deal Value * Probability of Closing = Weighted Deal Value`. This way, you can see how much potential revenue you're truly working with at any given moment.

Example: If you have a $10,000 deal in the negotiation stage with a 50% probability of closing, your spreadsheet would calculate: `10,000 * 0.50 = 5,000`. This means you can project $5,000 as a realistic pipeline value.

Step 2: Automate Insights

One of the best things about using spreadsheets for pipeline management is that you can automate a lot of insights and tracking. Automation helps you stay on top of your pipeline without manually checking every lead.

Conditional Formatting:

This allows you to highlight important cells based on certain conditions. For example:

- **Hot Leads**: If a lead is in the negotiation stage and has passed 30 days without movement, you can set it to turn red. This visual cue helps you identify leads that need immediate attention.
- **Upcoming Closures**: Deals that are expected to close within the next week can be highlighted in yellow to give them extra focus.

Example:

- If a deal has been sitting in the 'proposal' stage for over 15 days without progress, it turns yellow or red. This highlights the deal as needing follow-up.

Pro Tip: Regularly review your pipeline every week. As a sales leader, you should always have a good pulse on what's happening with each opportunity. Is there movement? Are deals getting stuck? The goal is to have a dynamic pipeline—your pipeline should evolve as fast as your prospects' needs.

Step 3: Visualize Your Progress

Tracking deals and seeing how you're progressing is just as important as managing them. Visualization tools like pivot tables and charts can help you analyze key performance indicators, identify bottlenecks, and determine which sales stages are working and which need improvement.

Pivot Tables:

A pivot table is a powerful tool for summarizing and analyzing large amounts of data. It can help you organize data by region, deal value, sales rep performance, etc. It's a game-changer when trying to see patterns and trends in your pipeline. For example, you can analyze the distribution of deals across different regions or assess which sales reps are closing the most deals in specific stages.

Charts and Graphs:

Visual representations of your data will give you an instant understanding of your pipeline. You could use bar charts to track the value of deals per region, line graphs to track deal progression over time, or pie charts to analyze the distribution of deals in various stages. These charts help you get a quick snapshot of where your team is focusing their efforts and where they need to adjust.

Pro Tip: Use visual insights to focus your energy where it will have the most impact. For example, if you see that many deals are stuck at the negotiation stage, it may be time to focus on improving that part of your sales process.

Real-World Example:

A South African SaaS startup, with a lean sales team, used Google Sheets to manage a pipeline of 300 leads. Initially, they lacked the budget for a CRM, so they manually tracked leads and deals through a custom-built spreadsheet. By using automation features like weighted values and conditional formatting, they were able to prioritize high-value leads and spot slow-moving deals. Over six months, they implemented visualizations to track progress by region, sales rep, and deal stage. This led to a 20% increase in close rates and helped them optimize their sales processes.

Key Takeaways:

- Spreadsheets, though simple, can be powerful tools for pipeline management in resource-constrained environments.
- Automation, using formulas and conditional formatting, can help you track and manage your pipeline more efficiently.
- Visualization tools like pivot tables and charts are invaluable for understanding performance at a glance.
- Regular reviews and updates to your pipeline are critical for maintaining momentum and identifying gaps in your sales strategy.

Next Steps:

As you scale your sales team, moving to more sophisticated tools like CRMs becomes a priority. However, the foundation of pipeline management should always rest on the principles you learn here: data accuracy, automation, and visualization. You can always build on this as your business grows, but for now, these steps will help you stay organized and focused on driving results.

Chapter 3: Scaling from One to 100 Salespeople

Scaling a sales team from one individual to a finely tuned machine of 100 high-performing professionals is a challenge that separates great leaders from the rest. This is where strategy meets grit, and vision must marry execution. The key to success lies in creating replicable systems, fostering a culture of excellence, and constantly sharpening the team's collective edge. Scaling isn't about chaos; it's about creating a deliberate rhythm that drives results, inspires trust, and sustains growth.

Step 1: Build a Strong Foundation

The foundation of any great sales team starts with the people who lay the first bricks. These early hires aren't just sales reps—they're architects. They create the blueprint for what the team will eventually become. At this stage, you're looking for generalists: versatile individuals who can handle prospecting, closing, and account management with equal zeal.

What to Look for in Early Hires:

- Adaptability: These individuals thrive in ambiguity and wear multiple hats effortlessly.
- Initiative: Early sales reps must be self-starters who can create their own playbook before one exists.
- Grit: Your first hires will shape your team's ethos. Choose people who embody grit, resilience, and a growth mindset.

Example: When Flutterwave launched in Nigeria, the first sales hires weren't just closing deals—they were educating customers, refining the product pitch, and identifying market gaps. Their work wasn't glamorous, but it laid the foundation for a sales machine that would later scale across Africa.

Action Plan:

1. Define Non-Negotiables: Identify the values and skills every hire must have, such as adaptability and a results-driven attitude.
2. Use Referrals: Early hires often come from trusted networks. Leverage your connections to find people who can hit the ground running.
3. Immerse Them in the Vision: These hires aren't just employees; they're co-builders. Share the mission and make them feel like stakeholders in the journey.

Step 2: Define Clear Metrics

As your team grows, metrics are the language of accountability. Without them, you're operating blind. Metrics turn gut feelings into actionable insights, providing a roadmap for performance improvement.

Key Metrics for Scaling:

1. Call Volume: Measures how actively your team is prospecting.
    - *Example*: An SDR making 60 calls a day has a better chance of creating opportunities than one making 20.
2. Pipeline Velocity: Tracks how quickly deals move through your sales stages.

- *Action*: If deals are stalling at the proposal stage, revisit the value proposition or pricing model.
3. Win Rate: The ratio of closed deals to total opportunities pursued.
   - *Insight*: A low win rate might point to poor lead qualification or ineffective objections handling.
4. Customer Acquisition Cost (CAC): Tracks how much it costs to acquire each new customer.
   - *Tip*: Optimize CAC by focusing on high-value prospects and automating repetitive tasks.

Pro Tip: Create a dashboard—whether in Excel or a CRM—that visualizes these metrics in real-time. Make performance transparent and discuss progress in weekly team meetings.

Step 3: Implement a Sales Playbook

A sales playbook isn't just a document—it's your team's operating system. It ensures consistency, reduces ramp-up time for new hires, and eliminates guesswork.

What Your Playbook Must Include:

1. Sales Stages with Criteria: Define each stage of the sales process and the specific actions required to move to the next. For example:
   - *Discovery*: Identify pain points, budget, and timeline.
   - *Proposal*: Present a customized solution and secure verbal buy-in.
   - *Negotiation*: Address pricing objections and finalize terms.

2. Scripts and Templates: Equip your team with tested cold-call scripts, email templates, and objection-handling strategies.
3. Buyer Personas: Detailed profiles of your ideal customers, including their challenges, decision-making processes, and KPIs.
4. Objection Handling Matrix: Common objections and tailored responses, ensuring reps are never caught off guard.

Case Study: When a South African SaaS company scaled from 5 to 30 reps, they introduced a playbook that standardized everything from discovery calls to closing techniques. Within a year, close rates improved by 25%, and reps onboarded in half the time.

Step 4: Specialize the Team

As your team grows, specialization becomes the secret sauce for efficiency. Generalists are great for startups, but specialists drive enterprise growth.

Specialized Roles to Introduce:

1. Sales Development Representatives (SDRs): Focus solely on lead generation and qualification.
2. Account Executives (AEs): Own the closing process, turning qualified leads into paying customers.
3. Customer Success Managers (CSMs): Handle post-sale relationships, ensuring retention and upselling opportunities.

Benefits of Specialization:

- Increased Productivity: SDRs can generate more leads, freeing AEs to focus on closing deals.
- Better Customer Experience: CSMs provide dedicated support, improving customer satisfaction and reducing churn.

Example:

When Flutterwave transitioned to specialized roles, their SDR team doubled the number of qualified leads, while AEs focused on closing deals worth $50,000+. This division of labor led to a 40% increase in revenue within 18 months.

Step 5: Invest in Leadership and Training

The difference between a good sales team and a great one often boils down to leadership. Scaling isn't just about hiring more reps; it's about creating leaders who can multiply your impact.

What Great Sales Leaders Do:

1. Coach Consistently: Conduct weekly 1-on-1s to review performance, address challenges, and provide tailored guidance.
2. Foster Accountability: Celebrate wins, but also dissect losses to identify gaps. Make improvement a team-wide focus.
3. Inspire with Vision: A leader's role isn't just to manage—it's to inspire. Keep your team aligned with the company's mission and show them how their work contributes to the bigger picture.

Real-World Example:

When a leading fintech company in Kenya scaled to 100 sales reps, they introduced a tiered leadership structure. Team leads conducted role-playing exercises and reviewed call recordings weekly. This approach didn't just improve performance—it created a culture of continuous learning.

Final Thoughts

Scaling a sales team from one to 100 isn't a sprint; it's a marathon. It requires a balance of art and science, vision and execution. By building a strong foundation, defining clear metrics, creating a robust playbook, specializing roles, and investing in leadership, you can turn your sales team into a revenue-generating powerhouse.

Scaling is hard, but remember this: greatness isn't built in comfort zones. Push yourself, push your team, and watch what happens when preparation meets opportunity. Africa's market is vast, its potential immense, and the future yours to conquer.

Chapter 4: Direct vs. Indirect Sales in Africa

Selling in Africa requires a deep understanding of the region's complexities and nuances. It's not a one-size-fits-all approach, especially when it comes to the methods you use to close deals. In Africa, we see two distinct approaches to sales: direct and indirect, each playing a crucial role in navigating the continent's diverse market landscape.

Direct Sales: Building Relationships and Securing High-Value Deals

Direct sales involve engaging prospects face-to-face or through personalized communication. It's a method that emphasizes relationship-building and personal trust. Direct sales are especially effective when you are dealing with complex, high-value deals that require a deeper connection with the buyer.

For example, Nigeria has a strong culture of personal relationships in business. In the corporate world, meetings often need to take place in person. It's not just about selling a product or service, but rather about developing trust over time. Many Nigerian business leaders prefer dealing with individuals they know personally or who have come highly recommended. In this case, direct sales become not just a way to make a sale, but a necessary method to open doors.

Key Factors for Direct Sales in Africa:

- **Trust and Relationship**: In many African countries, personal relationships are crucial. Decisions are often made based on trust and longstanding connections, rather than on price alone.

- **High-Touch Communication**: Sales professionals must engage with stakeholders one-on-one, listen to their needs, and present tailored solutions.
- **Local Understanding**: The ability to speak the local language or understand the local culture can be a huge advantage in direct sales. Buyers want to know that you understand their environment.

Example: In South Africa, a SaaS company selling financial software to banks may require a direct sales approach to engage with C-suite executives. These executives value in-person interactions, where trust can be developed and business concerns can be addressed in real-time. This approach would involve a lot of networking, attending industry events, and spending time with clients, often over the course of several months, to nurture relationships and close deals.

Pro Tip: In markets like Nigeria and South Africa, where face-to-face interaction is valued, allocate resources for business trips and networking events. This investment will pay off in the long run by fostering trust and helping you penetrate deeper into the market.

Indirect Sales: Scaling Quickly through Partnerships

While direct sales work well for high-value deals, the logistics and complexity of covering large regions with limited resources make it difficult to scale quickly. Enter indirect sales—a strategy that involves working with partners, resellers, or distributors to expand your reach without necessarily building a large in-house sales force.

In Kenya, for example, a local logistics startup partnered with regional distributors to reach rural markets. Without the need to build a costly internal sales team, the company increased its reach by 50% in less than a year. The success came from leveraging the local knowledge and established networks of distributors who could sell the product to a wider audience.

Key Benefits of Indirect Sales in Africa:

- **Reach and Scale**: By partnering with local businesses and distributors, you can rapidly expand your reach without the upfront investment of hiring a large sales team.
- **Local Expertise**: Partners have intimate knowledge of their local markets, and they can navigate cultural and logistical challenges that might otherwise slow down your expansion.
- **Cost-Efficiency**: You don't need to spend large sums on expanding your direct sales force. Instead, you can work with partners who already have customer bases and infrastructure in place.

Example: A tech company based in Kenya wanted to expand its customer base to the rural areas of East Africa. By partnering with telecom companies that already served these regions, the company was able to gain access to a large population and quickly scale its market presence. The partnership allowed the tech company to distribute their product at scale, without having to build a field sales team from scratch.

Pro Tip: When selecting partners, ensure they align with your values and objectives. Partners should not only be able to sell your product but also represent your brand in the marketplace.

Key Insight: The Hybrid Model

While both direct and indirect sales have their advantages, the hybrid model—leveraging the strengths of both strategies—is often the most effective approach for scaling in Africa.

A hybrid model allows you to build trust with a select group of clients through direct sales, while expanding rapidly across regions and markets using indirect sales methods. This balance enables you to meet the specific needs of high-value clients while also driving growth across a wider area through partnerships.

For example, if you are selling a cloud-based service across Africa, you could:

1. Use direct sales for enterprise accounts in larger cities where you can build personal relationships and tailor your solution to the unique needs of the business.
2. Use indirect sales to sell to small and medium-sized enterprises (SMEs) or remote areas, by partnering with local telecom companies or resellers who have existing relationships with customers.

Real-World Case Study: The Hybrid Approach

When M-Pesa, a mobile money service, first launched in Kenya, they initially used direct sales to engage businesses and high-value customers. However, their real success came from leveraging indirect sales through partnerships with mobile network providers, local agents, and banks. This allowed M-Pesa to quickly scale its offering to a broad base of customers across Kenya, and later to other African countries.

The success of M-Pesa demonstrates the power of combining direct and indirect sales. By directly engaging with key customers (businesses and high-net-worth individuals) and then leveraging partnerships to drive mass adoption, M-Pesa revolutionized mobile payments in Kenya and beyond.

Final Thoughts on Direct vs. Indirect Sales in Africa

The African market is vast, diverse, and presents a unique set of challenges. As a sales leader or entrepreneur, it's essential to understand when to use direct sales, when to use indirect sales, and how to blend both strategies into a cohesive plan.

- **Direct Sales** are ideal for high-value deals, requiring relationship-building and face-to-face interaction.
- **Indirect Sales** work best when you need to scale quickly, using partnerships and local networks.
- **The Hybrid Model** offers a balanced approach, combining trust-building and relationship management with the ability to scale rapidly.

The key to success is adaptability. Recognize the importance of both strategies and be prepared to switch between them depending on the market segment, the type of deal, and the available resources. The African sales landscape is evolving, and to thrive, sales leaders must remain agile, resourceful, and strategic.

Chapter 5: Leadership in Sales – Developing a Winning Team

Building a high-performing sales team isn't just about hiring the right people; it's about shaping them into leaders, innovators, and high-performers who can execute the vision you've laid out. In the African tech space, this is especially important because you'll be navigating markets that are still maturing. In many cases, you are selling innovation to regions that are leapfrogging traditional models. To succeed, you need to inspire your team to go beyond the ordinary and push boundaries.

Step 1: Establish a Vision and Culture of Excellence

A sales team needs a vision. Without it, they won't know where they're headed or why they're working hard to get there. Your vision should not only encompass sales targets but should also instill the values that will guide their actions. In Africa, where uncertainty can often dictate the pace of business, a clear, unwavering vision will keep the team focused and motivated.

For example, consider Jumia, Africa's leading e-commerce platform. In their early stages, Jumia's leadership understood the unique challenges they faced in building consumer trust in online retail across Africa. They crafted a vision that emphasized accessibility, local partnerships, and customer service excellence. This vision allowed their team to remain united and resilient even as they encountered challenges like payment processing and shipping logistics.

Step 2: Lead by Example

Sales leaders in Africa often have to be on the ground—meeting customers, attending events, and understanding the pulse of the market. When you show up for your team, they will follow your lead. The sales leader's presence is vital, especially in a region where personal relationships play a key role in business success.

Use real-world insights from companies like Paystack—whose founders worked tirelessly in the field to understand both merchants and consumers. They listened to their customers' needs, built relationships with financial institutions, and were relentless in improving their offering. As the leader, your presence should be felt in every deal and relationship your team builds.

Step 3: Implement a High-Performance Sales Process

A high-performance sales process involves more than just understanding the customer's needs—it requires an operational structure that supports both the customer and the sales team. Start by creating a robust sales playbook.

The Sales Playbook:

1. Lead Qualification: Define your ideal customer profile (ICP) and use data-driven insights to prioritize leads.
2. Sales Process Stages: Break down the sales journey into stages like qualification, nurturing, pitching, and closing.
3. Objection Handling: Create a list of common objections in the African market (e.g., pricing concerns, service reliability, payment options) and provide clear rebuttals.
4. Cross-Functional Collaboration: Ensure that your sales, marketing, and customer success teams are aligned. In Africa, collaboration across teams is crucial, as deals often require customization and deep understanding of the local context.

Step 4: Focus on Training and Development

Sales professionals in Africa are often stepping into roles that require them to be adaptable and resourceful. Ongoing training is a critical part of keeping the team aligned with changing market conditions.

Hold regular training sessions that focus on:

- Tech Adoption: Understanding new technological trends, especially in industries like fintech, mobile banking, and e-commerce.
- Customer-Centric Selling: Teach your team how to position products based on the specific needs and pain points of your customers.
- Negotiation Skills: In many African cultures, negotiation is an art form. Train your team to be flexible, yet firm, in their approach.

Pro Tip: Conduct role-playing exercises to simulate customer conversations. Focus on active listening and consultative selling. Sales teams should be able to pivot their approach based on the unique needs of each customer.

Real-World Example:

When Tala, a micro-lending platform, expanded into Kenya, they focused on building trust with a local sales team who deeply understood customer behavior. This approach paid off—within six months, Tala had successfully onboarded over 100,000 users. Their success was largely due to their team's ability to empathize with the market's needs and adjust their pitch accordingly.

Chapter 6: Selling with Data – Making Smart Decisions to Scale

Data isn't just a tool; it's your competitive edge. In the fast-paced African market, data empowers you to make smarter decisions, scale your efforts effectively, and pivot with precision when needed. While many view data as an abstract concept, in sales, it is the foundation of every successful strategy. This chapter dives deep into actionable steps to collect, analyze, and leverage data for unparalleled sales success.

Step 1: Collect the Right Data

Every successful data strategy begins with knowing what to measure. Collecting data for data's sake is a waste of time and resources. The key is to identify metrics that are both actionable and relevant to your market. For Africa, this means factoring in the continent's diversity and rapid change.

Core Metrics to Track:

1. **Customer Acquisition Cost (CAC):**
   - *Why It Matters*: In price-sensitive markets, keeping CAC low can determine profitability.
   - *How to Track*: Use tools like Google Analytics or HubSpot to calculate CAC for each region. For example, compare the cost of acquiring a customer in urban areas like Johannesburg versus rural markets in Kenya.

2. **Customer Lifetime Value (CLV):**
   - *Why It Matters*: CLV helps you focus on customers who bring the most value over time, guiding resource allocation.
   - *How to Track*: Segment customers by region or product and calculate average revenue per customer over their lifecycle.
3. **Conversion Rates:**
   - *Why It Matters*: Conversion rates highlight how effectively your sales funnel is working.
   - *How to Track*: Use Excel pivot tables or CRM tools to track the percentage of prospects that move through each sales stage.

Pro Tip: Don't overcomplicate your data collection process. Start simple. Use Google Sheets to create a manual dashboard if a CRM isn't feasible. Focus on a few key metrics and build from there.

Step 2: Analyze Your Data for Insights

Data without analysis is like a map without context—it shows you where you are but not where to go. The next step is to uncover patterns and actionable insights. Here's how:

Techniques for Data Analysis:

1. **Segment Your Data:** Break down your pipeline by geography, industry, or customer size.

- *Example*: A South African fintech startup might find that enterprise clients in Gauteng close faster than those in Cape Town, indicating a stronger need for tailored sales strategies.

2. **Visualize Trends:**

    Use bar graphs, pie charts, and heat maps to make patterns more visible.
    - *Example*: A heat map could reveal that inquiries spike in the last week of every quarter, allowing you to align your sales efforts with buying behavior.

3. **Identify Bottlenecks:**

    Use conditional formatting to flag deals stuck in the pipeline.
    - *Example*: Deals older than 30 days in the "Proposal Sent" stage might indicate pricing objections that need addressing.

Case Study:

A logistics company in Kenya analyzed their data to find that smaller clients required excessive hand-holding, while mid-sized businesses offered higher margins with fewer support requests. They refocused their sales efforts, leading to a 20% increase in revenue within six months.

Step 3: Use Data to Inform Strategy

Data analysis isn't the endgame—it's the beginning of actionable strategies that drive growth. The insights you gather should shape your decisions in real-time.

How to Apply Insights:

1. **Optimize Your Pipeline:**

    If you notice a particular stage in your sales process is slowing down conversions, revisit your approach.

    - *Example*: A telecom startup in Nigeria noticed deals stalled during the demo phase. After integrating a 15-minute "mini demo," their conversion rates increased by 30%.

2. **Refine Targeting:**

    Use your data to focus on high-value prospects.

    - *Example*: If customers in the fintech sector show a 60% higher CLV, allocate more resources to acquiring similar clients.

3. **Adapt to Regional Needs:**

    Leverage data to tailor strategies for specific regions.

    - *Example*: A SaaS company operating in Africa found that rural areas preferred offline-enabled solutions due to inconsistent internet access. By focusing on this feature in their pitch, they doubled their close rate.

Step 4: Tell a Story with Data

Data is only as powerful as your ability to communicate it. In sales, the story behind the numbers often closes the deal.

Steps to Crafting a Data-Driven Story:

1. **Start with the Problem:**

    Use your data to frame the customer's pain points.

    - *Example*: "We've noticed that 70% of businesses in your industry experience delayed payments due to inefficient billing systems."

2. **Show the Solution:**

    Demonstrate how your product addresses these pain points with data-driven proof.

    - *Example*: "Our platform reduces billing delays by 40%, saving businesses like yours $10,000 annually."

3. **End with Impact:**

    Use data to highlight the tangible outcomes.

    - *Example*: "Our clients have seen a 25% increase in on-time payments within three months of implementation."

Real-World Example: How Data Transformed Paystack

When Paystack entered the African market, they initially struggled to gain traction. By analyzing their sales data, they uncovered that small businesses in Lagos faced a unique challenge: inconsistent access to payment platforms. Armed with this insight, Paystack focused on reliability as their key selling point. They introduced features that ensured uptime even during power outages, which resonated deeply with their audience. The result? A 40% increase in adoption within the first year.

Pro Tip: Iterate Continuously. Data isn't static; it evolves. Make it a habit to review your data weekly and adapt accordingly. Set up regular feedback loops to ensure your strategies remain aligned with market realities.

Final Thoughts

Selling with data isn't just about numbers—it's about clarity, precision, and storytelling. It's about showing your team and your prospects that you're not guessing—you're making informed decisions. In a continent as dynamic as Africa, leveraging data effectively can be the difference between thriving and just surviving.

Now, go beyond the spreadsheet. Make data your weapon and scaling your reward.

Chapter 7: Building a Scalable Sales Process

As your sales team grows, so does the need for a standardized, repeatable process that fosters consistency and drives results. Without one, even the best sales talent risks becoming ineffective, navigating a chaotic path where opportunities are missed, deals stall, and customers lose confidence. In Africa, where the market landscape is diverse, resource allocation is critical, and trust takes precedence over flashy sales tactics, a scalable sales process is not just a tool—it's your lifeline.

Step 1: Define the Stages of Your Sales Process

Defining clear stages in your sales funnel provides the foundation for everything else. In Africa, this often requires adapting traditional sales methodologies to fit regional nuances, such as face-to-face engagements, local pricing strategies, and infrastructure challenges.

Your Scalable Sales Funnel:

1. **Lead Generation:**

    Leads are the lifeblood of your funnel. Whether sourced through inbound strategies like referrals or website inquiries, or outbound techniques like cold calling, every lead needs to be documented and categorized. For example, in the Kenyan market, word-of-mouth referrals often yield high-quality leads, making networking events essential for B2B players.

2. **Qualification:**

    Not all leads are created equal. Create criteria to qualify leads based on budget, authority, need, and timeline (BANT). In South Africa's mature financial market, for instance, a decision-maker with a clear budget and timeline is more likely to close quickly.

3. **Presentation:**

    Presenting your solution effectively is where you win or lose deals. African buyers often approach technology with skepticism, so demonstrating the tangible impact of your product—whether through ROI examples or hands-on demos—is critical. Tie your pitch to local pain points like cost efficiency, scalability, or overcoming infrastructure challenges.

4. **Proposal & Negotiation:**

    Crafting the right proposal involves aligning your pricing with market realities. Be flexible enough to accommodate local practices, such as installment payments in regions where upfront capital might be scarce. For example, a SaaS company offering pricing in local currency gains a competitive edge.

5. **Closing:**

    This stage requires a personal touch. Face-to-face meetings often seal deals in markets like Nigeria, where relationships are central to business success. Show adaptability and remain patient, as decisions may involve multiple stakeholders.

6. **Post-Sale Follow-Up:**

    Retention drives growth. After closing the deal, check in regularly to ensure the client is getting value and identify upsell opportunities. For example, a logistics firm might offer training sessions to help their clients use new tracking software effectively.

Step 2: Train Your Team on the Sales Process

Scaling your sales team means every member must execute consistently, without reinventing the wheel. A standardized process ensures alignment while still allowing flexibility for local nuances.

The Sales Playbook: Your playbook should be the central document that every team member can reference. It must include:

- **Lead Qualification Criteria:**

  Define what constitutes a "hot" lead. For example, a lead with decision-making authority in an Ethiopian telecommunications firm might be considered high-priority if they've expressed a need for cost optimization.

- **Cold Calling Scripts & Email Templates:**

  Equip your team with tools to reach out confidently. For instance, create an email template that emphasizes ROI for industries like healthcare or logistics.

- **Objection Handling Techniques:**

  Address common concerns, such as pricing or implementation timelines, by providing rebuttals. E.g., "Our phased deployment ensures minimal disruption to your operations."

- **Metrics for Success:**

  Focus on KPIs like time-to-close and customer satisfaction scores, aligning performance with business outcomes.

Real-World Example:

A fintech startup in Ghana trained its initial sales team with weekly role-playing exercises based on the playbook. Within six months, their time-to-close reduced by 20%, and the team became more adept at addressing complex objections.

Step 3: Use Technology to Automate and Optimize

Technology doesn't replace your team; it amplifies their efforts. For African sales teams with limited resources, choosing cost-effective, impactful tools is key.

Affordable Tech Stack:

1. **Google Sheets or Airtable:**
   Use these to create basic CRM systems. Track lead progress, calculate weighted pipeline values, and flag overdue deals.
2. **Zoho CRM or HubSpot Free Tier:**
   Ideal for managing more complex pipelines and automating follow-ups.
3. **Visualization Tools:**
   Dashboards in tools like Google Data Studio help visualize performance by region or rep.

Actionable Automation:

- Automate follow-ups with pre-written email sequences for leads in the proposal stage.
- Set alerts for deals that remain in a stage longer than average, ensuring timely intervention.
- Use AI-driven tools like Gong.io for call analysis, helping reps improve their pitch.

Pro Tip:

Review dashboards weekly to monitor metrics like conversion rates and bottlenecks. Encourage reps to take ownership of their data and continuously refine their approach.

Step 4: Consistently Review and Improve

Markets evolve—so should your sales process. Schedule regular reviews to assess what's working and what's not.

Data-Driven Improvement:

- Analyze which deals close fastest and replicate those strategies.
- Solicit feedback from your sales team to identify friction points in the process.
- Use customer insights to refine your messaging, ensuring it resonates with evolving needs.

Real-World Example:

A South African SaaS firm noticed a drop in conversions during their demo stage. By reviewing their data, they discovered that demos were too generic. After customizing demos for industries like retail and manufacturing, their demo-to-close rate increased by 25%.

Final Thoughts

Scaling from one to 100 salespeople isn't about finding superstars—it's about creating a system that allows good salespeople to perform exceptionally well. Build a strong foundation, invest in training, leverage technology, and continuously refine your process. Success in Africa's dynamic markets demands both structure and adaptability, but with the right approach, your team can scale faster and more effectively than you ever imagined.

Chapter 8: Building Relationships – The Heart of African Sales

In Africa, sales success is deeply rooted in relationships. This is not a market where you can rely solely on transactional methods or flashy marketing campaigns. Instead, African sales demand patience, trust-building, and a genuine commitment to understanding the cultural and business dynamics at play. Relationships are the foundation upon which long-term success is built, and nurturing them requires strategy, empathy, and a multi-touch approach.

Step 1: Start with Trust

Trust is the cornerstone of every business relationship in Africa. Unlike in many Western markets, where speed and efficiency often trump personal connections, African buyers prioritize knowing and trusting who they are doing business with before making decisions.

How to Build Trust:

1. **Listen Before You Pitch:**

    Start by asking questions about their business challenges, goals, and vision. This approach signals that you are genuinely interested in solving their problems, not just selling a product.

2. **Invest in Personal Interactions:**

    Phone calls, coffee meetings, and attending local community events can go a long way in establishing rapport. In regions like East Africa, a face-to-face meeting is often a prerequisite for closing deals.

3. **Leverage Recommendations:**

    In tight-knit business communities, personal recommendations and introductions carry significant weight. Secure referrals from respected individuals or organizations within the industry to establish credibility.

Example:

A South African IT firm entering the Kenyan market successfully onboarded its first clients by attending local industry meetups and building personal connections with key decision-makers. Over six months, these initial meetings snowballed into lasting relationships that drove recurring business.

Step 2: Master the Art of Multi-Touch Negotiation

Negotiation in Africa is as much about relationship-building as it is about reaching an agreement. It's a process that may involve multiple touchpoints, patience, and adaptability.

Keys to Effective Negotiation:

1. **Understand Cultural Nuances:**

    In Nigeria, bargaining is a cultural norm, so expect multiple rounds of back-and-forth discussions. In contrast, in countries like Botswana, negotiations may focus more on trust and relationship-building over price.

2. **Provide Transparency:**

    Transparency in pricing and deliverables demonstrates integrity, a trait highly valued in African markets. Be upfront about timelines, potential challenges, and costs.

3. **Focus on Win-Win Solutions:**

    Show your willingness to collaborate and tailor solutions to meet both parties' needs. This builds goodwill and sets the stage for a long-term relationship.

Example:

A Ghanaian agricultural technology company negotiated a partnership with local farmers' cooperatives by offering flexible payment terms and training workshops. By aligning their solution with the farmers' financial cycles, they secured a deal that increased their market share by 30%.

Step 3: Offer Value Beyond the Sale

The relationship doesn't end when the contract is signed. African buyers value partners who stay engaged, providing ongoing support, insights, and opportunities to grow together.

Post-Sale Relationship Building:

1. **Follow-Up Consistently:**

    Schedule regular check-ins to ensure your solution is delivering value and address any emerging issues.

2. **Share Insights:**

    Provide data, trends, or best practices relevant to your client's industry. This positions you as a trusted advisor, not just a vendor.

3. **Upsell Without Pressure:**

    Introduce additional products or services only when they genuinely solve a customer pain point.

Real-World Example:

M-Pesa, Kenya's leading mobile money service, solidified its market dominance by offering workshops to educate customers on new features. This proactive approach not only improved customer retention but also encouraged word-of-mouth referrals, resulting in a 10% annual growth rate.

Step 4: Use Strategic Partnerships to Strengthen Relationships

In Africa, strategic partnerships can amplify your ability to build meaningful connections and scale your efforts. These collaborations provide access to new networks and increase credibility.

How to Build Strategic Partnerships:

1. **Identify Key Influencers:**

    Collaborate with local influencers, industry leaders, or community organizations that resonate with your target audience.

2. **Prioritize Alignment:**

    Choose partners whose values and offerings complement yours. For instance, a SaaS company might partner with a telecom provider to bundle services for mutual clients.

3. **Deliver Mutual Value:**

    Partnerships thrive when both parties benefit. Structure agreements that clearly define shared objectives, such as co-marketing initiatives or revenue-sharing models.

Example:

A Nigerian HR software startup partnered with a regional HR association to offer free training at industry conferences. This partnership boosted brand visibility and credibility, resulting in a 40% increase in inbound leads over six months.

Step 5: Track Relationship Impact

To measure the effectiveness of your relationship-building efforts, it's essential to track their impact on your sales performance.

How to Track Relationships:

1. **Use a Relationship Tracker:**

    In tools like Google Sheets or CRM systems, track the following:
    - Number of touchpoints per client.
    - Time spent building rapport before closing a deal.
    - Customer satisfaction scores post-sale.

2. **Evaluate Conversion Rates:**

    Compare the close rates for leads where relationships were prioritized versus transactional approaches.

3. **Monitor Retention Metrics:**

    Track repeat purchases, upsells, and contract renewals to gauge the long-term value of your relationships.

Pro Tip: Assign a relationship strength score to each client, based on factors like frequency of communication, responsiveness, and trust levels. Use this score to prioritize high-value relationships for deeper engagement.

Final Thoughts

In Africa, relationships are not just a "nice-to-have"; they are the currency of business. By investing time and energy into building trust, mastering negotiations, delivering ongoing value, leveraging partnerships, and tracking your efforts, you create a foundation for long-term success. Remember, it's not about selling a product—it's about becoming a trusted partner in your customers' growth journeys.

Chapter 9: Tracking Success – Metrics That Matter

Metrics are the lifeblood of any sales team. As you scale your sales operation in Africa, tracking success becomes more critical than ever. In a continent as diverse as Africa, with varying cultures, economic climates, and infrastructural challenges, identifying and tracking the right metrics ensures your team is moving in the right direction. This chapter will help you define success, set up a system to track metrics on a zero budget, and use data to tell compelling stories to executives.

Step 1: Define What Success Looks Like

Success in sales is not just about hitting revenue targets; it's about creating a sustainable and scalable sales engine. This involves defining quantitative and qualitative measures of success:

1. **Revenue Metrics:**
    - **Total Revenue:** The total earnings generated over a specific period.
    - **Average Deal Size:** A reflection of the value of each sale.
    - **Monthly Recurring Revenue (MRR):** Especially important for SaaS companies.
2. **Customer Metrics:**
    - **Customer Retention Rate:** Measures how well you're keeping your customers.
    - **Customer Satisfaction Score (CSAT):** Gauges how happy customers are with your product or service.
3. **Pipeline Metrics:**
    - **Lead Conversion Rate:** Tracks how many leads turn into paying customers.

- **Sales Cycle Length:** Measures the time it takes to close a deal from initial contact.
4. **Activity Metrics:**
    - **Calls or Meetings Booked Per Day:** Shows the effort sales reps are putting in.
    - **Emails Sent and Response Rates:** Tracks outreach effectiveness.

Example: A South African fintech startup set its success metric as a 20% increase in retention within 12 months. By focusing on this metric, the company improved its customer service and reduced churn by implementing personalized onboarding.

Step 2: Use KPIs to Drive Team Performance

Key Performance Indicators (KPIs) are the backbone of tracking team and individual performance. Here's how to set and align KPIs with your company's objectives:

1. **Daily KPIs:** Focus on actions that build pipeline momentum.
    - Example: Number of cold calls or emails sent.
2. **Weekly KPIs:** Reflect mid-term progress.
    - Example: Number of meetings booked or attended.
3. **Monthly KPIs:** Align with broader business goals.
    - Example: Total deals closed or revenue generated.

Tracking Hack for Teams with Zero Budget:

Use Google Sheets or Excel to create a shared KPI tracker. Each salesperson should update their metrics daily, and the sheet can automatically calculate totals, averages, and trends using formulas like =SUM() and =AVERAGE(). Conditional formatting can highlight progress or gaps.

Step 3: Build an Excel Dashboard to Visualize Metrics

Visualizing data transforms raw numbers into insights that drive decisions. Here's how to create a simple yet powerful Excel dashboard:

1. **Start with Clean Data:**

   - Use separate tabs for raw data, calculated metrics, and charts.
   - Ensure consistency by using drop-down lists for categories like "Lead Source" or "Deal Stage."

2. **Set Up Key Visualizations:**

   - **Pipeline Health:** Use a stacked bar chart to show leads at each stage of the funnel.
   - **Revenue Trends:** A line graph can depict revenue growth over time.
   - **Conversion Rates:** A pie chart can break down conversions by lead source or region.

3. **Automate Insights:**

   - Use formulas like =IF() to flag stalled deals. For example, flag deals that have been in the same stage for more than 30 days.

    o Use pivot tables to analyze performance by region, sales rep, or product line.

Example Visualization:

- A Nigerian SaaS company created a pipeline health dashboard using Google Sheets. They used conditional formatting to flag deals older than 60 days and pie charts to display lead sources. This approach increased their pipeline velocity by 15% in a quarter.

Step 4: Use Metrics to Inform Strategy

Collecting data is just the beginning. The real magic lies in analyzing it to inform your strategy and telling a compelling story to stakeholders. Here's how:

1. **Spot Trends:**

    Identify patterns in the data. Are certain regions underperforming? Are specific sales reps excelling in closing deals? Use these insights to make informed adjustments.

2. **Identify Bottlenecks:**

    If deals are stalling in a particular stage, investigate why. Are reps struggling with negotiations? Are follow-ups inconsistent? Once you pinpoint the issue, implement targeted training or tools to address it.

3. **Set Goals and Benchmarks:**

    Use historical data to set realistic benchmarks for future performance. For example, if your average close rate is 30%, set a goal of improving to 35% over the next quarter.

4. **Tell the Story:**

   Data should be presented in a way that's easy to understand and actionable. Use the following framework to tell the story:

   - **The Problem:** Highlight challenges, such as a drop in conversion rates.
   - **The Insight:** Show the data trends that reveal why the problem exists.
   - **The Solution:** Recommend actions, like increasing training for objection handling or targeting a new segment.

Case Study: A Kenyan logistics startup faced declining win rates in their rural markets. By analyzing their data, they discovered that internet connectivity issues were stalling their follow-ups. Armed with this insight, they introduced offline capabilities in their software, resulting in a 25% increase in rural sales.

Step 5: Track Relationships as a Metric

Building relationships is integral to sales success in Africa, so it's vital to track them effectively. Use these tactics:

1. **Create a Relationship Tracker:**

- Add a "Relationship Strength" column in your spreadsheet, rated on a scale of 1-10.
- Track touchpoints, such as meetings, follow-up emails, or referrals.

2. **Measure Relationship Impact:**

    - Track conversion rates for leads with strong relationships compared to cold outreach.
    - Monitor the lifetime value (LTV) of customers with deep engagements versus those acquired transactionally.

3. **Report Progress to Executives:**

    - Highlight how relationship-building efforts impact metrics like retention, upselling, and market penetration.
    - Use qualitative examples to complement quantitative data.

Final Thoughts

Tracking success in African sales goes beyond monitoring numbers—it's about understanding the stories behind the data. By leveraging tools like Excel and Google Sheets, even teams with limited budgets can gain actionable insights. When paired with thoughtful analysis and storytelling, these insights not only improve performance but also open up new markets and opportunities.

Remember: In sales, what gets measured gets managed. Use your data to not only track progress but to inspire innovation, drive growth, and scale your team to new heights.

Chapter 10: Structuring the Sales Process and Handling Objections – A Complete Blueprint for Success

Scaling and managing a sales team in Africa requires more than charisma and effort—it demands a structured, repeatable process and an ability to overcome objections effectively. Together, these elements create a winning strategy to navigate the complexities of the African market while fostering trust, improving efficiency, and driving revenue.

Your sales process is the backbone of your team's efforts. It's the compass that guides every interaction and ensures no deal falls through the cracks. A well-structured sales process includes clearly defined stages, measurable criteria, and ongoing data analysis to ensure it evolves with market demands.

Step 1: Define Your Sales Stages

Sales stages serve as milestones in the buyer's journey. For African markets, these stages must align with regional realities, including long decision-making cycles and relationship-focused negotiations. Here's a tailored structure:

1. **Lead Generation:**

    Gather prospects from events, referrals, inbound inquiries, or outbound efforts like cold emails and calls. In Africa, referrals and personal introductions are often more effective than digital campaigns.

Checklist:
- Has the lead expressed interest in your solution?
- Is there a clear business need?

2. **Lead Qualification:**

   Not every lead is worth pursuing. Assess their fit based on factors like budget, authority, need, and timeline (BANT).

   Checklist:
   - Do they meet the BANT criteria?
   - Have you identified the decision-makers?

3. **Needs Assessment:**

   Dive deeper into the customer's challenges. This stage sets the foundation for your value proposition.

   Checklist:
   - Have you mapped out their pain points?
   - Have you uncovered all stakeholders involved?

4. **Proposal & Negotiation:**

   Present a tailored solution, address objections, and negotiate terms. Keep flexibility in mind, as African markets often demand creative solutions like payment plans or phased rollouts.

5. **Closing:**

   Finalize the deal with signed agreements, onboarding, and clear post-sale follow-up plans.

Step 2: Criteria for Progression Between Stages

Each stage should have a checklist of criteria that must be met before moving forward. This ensures consistency and reduces wasted effort.

For example:

- **From Lead Generation to Qualification:**
  Ensure the lead has expressed a tangible need for your product.
- **From Proposal to Closing:**
  Verify that all objections have been addressed and that the decision-maker is fully aligned.

Step 3: Using Data to Optimize Your Pipeline

Tracking data isn't optional—it's essential. Use tools like Google Sheets or low-cost CRMs to monitor your pipeline, even if you're a startup with no budget.

1. **Track KPIs:**
   - Conversion rates by stage.
   - Average deal size.
   - Time spent in each stage.

2. **Create Dashboards:**

   Use pivot tables to visualize bottlenecks. For example, if deals are stalling in the negotiation stage, investigate common objections.

3. **Analyze Trends:**

   Are certain regions outperforming others? Is a specific product more appealing? Use this information to refine your strategy.

In sales, objections are inevitable. They're not roadblocks but opportunities to address concerns, educate your customer, and strengthen your value proposition.

Step 1: Understand the Root Cause

Objections usually fall into these categories:

- **Pricing:** "Your product is too expensive."
- **Product Fit**: "I'm not sure this will solve our problem."
- **Trust:** "I've never heard of your company."

The key is to dig deeper. Use open-ended questions like, "Can you help me understand what's holding you back?"

Step 2: Create a Playbook for Common Objections

Prepare your team with scripts and responses for the most frequent objections.

1. **Pricing:**
    - Highlight ROI. For instance, if your product saves the customer 20% in operational costs, emphasize how they'll recoup their investment.
    - Offer flexible terms or phased implementations.
2. **Product Fit:**
    - Use case studies to show how similar customers benefited.
    - Offer trial periods to demonstrate the product's effectiveness.
3. **Trust:**
    - Provide references or testimonials from other clients.
    - Share details about your company's track record and industry expertise.

Step 3: Track Objections and Outcomes

Use your CRM or spreadsheet to log objections by stage and analyze patterns. For example:

- Are objections more common in certain regions?
- Which objections are you least successful in overcoming?

Actionable Tip:

If "pricing" is the most common objection, consider bundling your services to offer more value at the same cost.

Step 4: The Power of Multi-Touch Relationships

Building trust in African markets often requires multiple touchpoints:

- **Face-to-Face Meetings:** Crucial for high-value deals.
- **Follow-Up Emails:** Reinforce your message with data or additional insights.
- **Community Engagement:** Participate in local events to establish your brand's presence.

Metrics to Track Success

1. **Objection Conversion Rate:**

   Measure how often your team turns objections into sales.

2. **Time to Resolution:**

   Track how quickly your team addresses objections.

3. **Lost Deals Analysis:**

   For every lost deal, record the primary objection and brainstorm solutions.

Final Thoughts

Combining a structured sales process with an objection-handling strategy sets your team up for long-term success. By defining clear stages, criteria, and metrics, you create a scalable system that adapts to the complexities of African markets. At the same time, mastering the art of overcoming objections ensures that no deal is left on the table without a fight.

When you blend process and resilience, your sales team doesn't just grow—it thrives. This combination transforms your organization into a revenue-driving powerhouse capable of navigating the unique challenges and opportunities of selling in Africa.

www.ingramcontent.com/pod-product-compliance
Lightning Source LLC
Chambersburg PA
CBHW070958240526
45469CB00017B/2444